AF271688

Edited by Hollay Ghadery
Rasiqra Revulva
& Amanda Shankland

SPEECH DRIES HERE ON THE TONGUE

Poetry on Environmental Collapse and Mental Health

Cover image by TheAlchemi4st
Cover and book design by Jeremy Luke Hill
Proofread by Mary Hamilton
Set in Linux Libertine and Open Sans
Printed on Coach House Laid
Printed and bound by Arkay Design & Print

LIBRARY AND ARCHIVES CANADA CATALOGUING IN PUBLICATION

Title: Speech dries here on the tongue : poetry on environmental collapse and
    mental health / edited by Hollay Ghadery, Rasiqra Revulva, & Amanda
    Shankland.
Names: Ghadery, Hollay, editor. | Revulva, Rasiqra, 1985- editor | Shankland,
    Amanda, editor.
Identifiers: Canadiana (print) 20250158450 | Canadiana (ebook) 20250159473 |
    ISBN 9780889844902 (softcover) | ISBN 9780889844926 (EPUB) |
    ISBN 9780889844919 (PDF)
Subjects: LCSH: Canadian poetry—21st century. | CSH: Canadian poetry
    (English)— 21st century. | LCSH: Environmental degradation—Health
    aspects—Poetry. | LCSH: Mental health—Environmental aspects—Poetry. |
    LCGFT: Ecopoetry. | LCGFT: Poetry.
Classification: LCC PS8293.1 .S656 2025 | DDC C811/.608036—dc23

The Porcupine's Quill gratefully acknowledges the support of the Canada Council for the Arts, the Ontario Arts Council, and the Ontario Book Publishing Tax Credit.

The Porcupine's Quill respectfully acknowledges the ancestral homelands of the Attawandaron, Anishinaabe, Haudenosaunee, and Métis Peoples, and recognizes that we are situated on Treaty 3 territory, the traditional territory of Mississaugas of the Credit First Nation.

The Porcupine's Quill also recognizes and supports the diverse persons who make up its community, regardless of race, age, culture, ability, ethnicity, nationality, gender identity and expression, sexual orientation, marital status, religious affiliation, and socioeconomic status.

The Porcupine's Quill
130 Dublin Street North
Guelph, Ontario, Canada
N1H 4N4
www.porcupinesquill.ca

Table of Contents

Gary Barwin & Elee Kraljii Gardiner

gregor Y kennedy

Aaron Kreuter

Concetta Principe

AJ Dolman

Tara McGowan-Ross

D.A. Lockhart

Conal Smiley

Editors' Preface

In an age of unprecedented environmental crises, honouring diverse experiences means acknowledging the many ways people connect with and respond to the state of the world. Emily Dickinson famously wrote that "hope is the thing with feathers," it is light and gentle but persistent and sustains our will to act. Others may find hope elusive, weighed down by grief and despair, as they witness the relentless toll of pollution, war, and ecocide. Wars in Gaza and Sudan leave us winded, shattered, devoid of hope. This interplay between hope and despair speaks to another important truth: how we treat each other is deeply connected to how we treat the natural world. If we are willing to harm one another for personal or political gain, environmental harm seems inevitable.

Yet, even amidst the destruction, we retain agency—we can choose who we want to be. Poetry can serve as a space to envision alternative futures, creating room for collective dreaming and transformation. This vision must also accommodate those for whom hope feels inaccessible, making space for the essential work of embracing pain, grief, and anger. But hope itself is not an uncomplicated remedy; it can be used to pacify or to shift blame from powerful entities onto individuals, as we see in eco-fascist narratives that hold ordinary people responsible for environmental degradation rather than the corporations fuelling it. In this way, hope can sometimes become a tool for maintaining the status quo, obstructing meaningful change.

Our collective experiences of the natural world have also evolved. Where once writers in the Romantic era focused on personal reverence for nature, today, social media and global connectivity allow environmental events to affect us communally. Disasters like Hurricane Katrina underscored how governments can fail marginalized communities; people watched in horror as the powerless were abandoned, dehumanized by the media, and neglected by those in power. Such failures are clear examples of environmental racism. In so-called Canada, the lack of clean drinking water on Indigenous reserves and industrial pollution in low-income neighbourhoods reminds us that our situation is not so different than our neighbours to the south.

Across the world, people are grieving the state of the environment. In British Columbia, emergency doctors have reported a rise in climate-related anxiety and suicides, especially after events like the wildfires that devastated Lytton and impacted Kamloops. In Northern Canada, environmental collapse has disrupted traditional ways of life for the Inuit, contributing to one of the highest suicide rates in the world. Although these are extreme cases, they highlight how common depression and anxiety about environmental decline and climate change have become.

The eco-fascist ideologies that compound these injustices suggest that ordinary people are the problem, subtly disempowering us from realizing our potential to drive change. This alienation deepens the divide between people and nature. Indigenous perspectives, however, remind us that humans are integral to natural systems and can be guardians of ecological balance. As Native American poet Joy Harjo writes, "We are all related, and we come from the same sacred place. We are part of the land, not separate from it. The earth breathes us, and we breathe the earth."

In a world driven by capitalist exploitation, exhaustion becomes both a product and a tool. People depleted by environmental and social crises become more compliant consumers, filling the void with work and consumption rather than family, community, knowledge, and human connection. This relentless cycle erodes our capacity to build authentic connections. In such a world, simply sharing a home-cooked meal together becomes both an act of disobedience and a symbol of our capacity to restore unity through being together.

Against this backdrop, art opens possibilities for imagining alternatives, inviting us to reimagine our relationships with each other and with the Earth. Therapy alone cannot address the institutional violence and environmental degradation we face. Instead, we must find ways to connect within, outside, and in opposition to the system—to support each other as we grapple with the challenges of this age and explore what it means to care for one another in a world where basic needs, like health, are treated as privileges rather than rights.

The concept for this book emerged during the COVID-19 pandemic, a time of deep isolation and hardship. As a means of coping, long walks in nature became a refuge. Many people struggle with depression and anxiety, particularly those living in urban environments where the disconnect from nature is palpable. The constant noise, light pollution, and ongoing environmental and water pollution are daily challenges. Several poems in this collection explore how individuals navigate the emotional and psychological toll of urban living, both consciously and unconsciously. The book aimed to bring together poets who share these struggles, fostering connections with others who have similar experiences. This naturally led to a focus on Indigenous poetry, as many Indigenous voices have documented their transitions from living in nature to grappling with the anxieties of modern, industrialized cities.

The poets in this book explore the complex relationship between environmental collapse and mental health, inviting readers to consider the unprecedented personal impacts of the crisis. The looming threat of environmental collapse has brought with it a sense of impending annihilation and intensified a mental health crisis that was made crueller by a global pandemic that revealed our fragile nature. As writers, we use our words to navigate this turmoil, alleviate our own suffering, and inspire others. Through speaking and writing, we reclaim power, not only over our own narratives but in how we shape our collective futures. As we continue to grapple with the overwhelming realities of ecological destruction, these poems invite us to listen, to feel, and to respond. In this moment of profound loss, we are reminded that the voice can be a force for change, a means of healing. Though the weight of environmental collapse may sometimes silence us, we are called to speak. Even as speech may dry on the tongue, it gives us a thirst for change.

Introduction, by Karen Houle

Gentle Reader, we are going to think together about mental health and poetry by beginning with a story about a Rubber Plant that didn't even belong to me.

The Rubber Plant belonged to a person named Sean. I barely knew him. He had heard one of my talks on activism and caretaking of soil and plants. He got in touch with me through a friend. He was very worried about his rubber plant. It lived on a dining room table in a house on a street off Stone Road in Guelph. He sent me a picture with a note: "Help! It's dying. It makes me so sad to see it like this."

Evidently, the plant was not doing well.

And, evidently, Sean's own well-being was connected to that.

Truth: no amount of watering more or watering less, or moving into more light or moving away from the light, would perk it up. It was dying. Sean was right. And once it died, he would, like a million other people, just have put it in the bin and forgotten about it so that he wouldn't be negatively affected anymore by the ill-health of a simple house plant.

But he didn't let it die. He called me. And we got together. And we triaged the plant. Now the plant is fine.

Let's think through together how radical and healing (for all) that unusual collective behaviour is.

Truth: Like any living being, a houseplant can be, or appear to be, healthy for a stretch of time after it is purchased. It's growing taller! Yay! It's putting out new leaves! Yay! It has flowers! Yay! A few cycles of boom and bust repeat. The soil looks healthy. It all looks happy there in the window: your little oasis of green plant, oxygen, soil, water, sunlight. A working ecology. A patch of heaven. Maybe it's all the garden you will ever have.

Then, like any living being, it can start to look a bit sick. It changes colour slightly: the waxy verdant green or stop-sign red fading to a less vibrant hue. Green turning toward yellow.

Brown turning toward black. Its leaves droop and fall off. Some leaves appear to have been eaten by a creature you had no idea shared your home: Are those mouse teeth marks?! Gross, sticky bugs are underneath the leaves and up the stem. Smaller bugs fly around it and up your nose and land in your tea. It just seems, well, less happy.

Those who are living around this unthriving being—you, the bugs, the rodents, other roommates hitherto unaccounted for—might feel:

a) Nothing. Zip. "Who cares? It's a plant!";

b) Frustration. Irritation. "Now I'll have to get a new one!"; or,

c) Concerned. Concerned in the way that one can feel concern for any other living being around us who is apparently not doing well.

Depending upon the emotional reaction of the houseplant "owner" (caretaker? foster parent? steward?) the following actions can be taken:

Before I lay out these choices, I want to reassure you that we are on track for an introduction for an anthology of poetry about mental health and climate chaos.

a) Put the dying plant in a basement or an unheated garage or directly outside onto the porch or driveway, even in the snow, yes, to make it die quicker and get it out of sight. Then, in the spring, throw it out. Remove the plastic or ceramic pot and throw the plant onto the garden. Or into the compost bin. Or maybe into the municipal green bin. Or over the fence into the brownfields beside the railway tracks. Or that cedar grove just beside the off-leash area by Victoria Road. Heck, don't even bother removing the plastic pot and hanger bits. Just get rid of it. It's dead or almost dead anyhow.

b) Time to go shopping! Get in a private vehicle (or taxi, or bus, or walk, or bike; doable but c'mon! very less likely!) and drive to Walmart or Home Depot or Canadian Tire. Buy a new Rubber Plant ($46.98 for a 21 cm pot). Go out to your car in the parking lot with the plant in a plastic sleeve for protection. (It could be in shock! From warm Costa Rican fields, to an airplane, to a rack in Home Depot in the winter!) Drive home. Put the new Rubber Plant in the spot where the other one was. Who will ever know?

c) It's triage time! Drive to Walmart or Home Depot or Canadian Tire. Buy houseplant fertilizer (Liquid All Purpose Miracle-Gro, $13.00) and the smallest possible bag of potting soil (8.8 L Miracle-Gro, $4.50). Throw in some mice (& god help us, rat) poison while you're at it (Tomcat Blue Maxx, $13.00). Go out to your car. Drive home. Take the ill plant out of the pot, put it onto some newspaper on that dining room table. Shake the old soil into the dustbin or composter and replace with new potting soil. Water. (What you are going to do with that newspaper now. Is it dirty? Wet? Can you start a fire with it? Dear me!) In about a month you can start using that liquid fertilizer. Administer regularly according to the instructions on the package so that your plant lasts longer. Or doesn't die as quickly. (Careful! It is the exact shade of blue of your "rodenticide".)

How are you feeling?
Have any other questions arisen for you in this plant tale? They have for me. Here are some: Where was this potting soil "made"? Where was the plastic bag that held the "Miracle-Gro" soil made? Where was the fertilizer made, and out of what? I see it has "fish protein" in it. Where were these "fish" from? How did they get into the factory where the blue liquid was made? Where was the plastic bottle made? And the clever dropper with the gradients on the side and the black rubber stopper? Where was the sticky label made? Where was this small disposable box that I bought it in, made? Then: How did the liquid get into the plastic bottle and the sticker onto the bottle and the bottle into the box and the box onto the shelf at Walmart or Home Depot in Guelph where I purchased it? Who or what did those steps? If it was a who, were they paid a living wage to oversee the automaton filling plastic bottles with blue liquid? To drive a shipment across the continent and unload massive cardboard boxes from a truck on a loading dock on night shift? Where will I put the fertilizer bottle and dropper when it is empty? And the plastic bag that the potting soil was in when I've used all the potting soil? And all those questions reapplied to the rodenticide plus the squirm-inducing one: What will

*I do with a dead mouse or rat? Into the grey waste bin and off to the
landfill for you, Sonny!*

*Sorry. These are just some of the considerations that typically
do not arise when considering the well-being of a single houseplant
in 2025 near Stone Road in Guelph.*

How are you feeling now? Tell me. Don't bottle it up.

d) Go out to the composter and dig out a paper bagful. Lift the
sad Rubber Plant gently out of the pot. Put plant, soil and all,
directly into the worm farm bin that lives under your dining room
table. No need for a newspaper. With your hands, massage the
"spent" potting soil out from around the root ball and let it fall
into the worm bin. (The worms will chew on it and spit it out as
healthy soil again). With the same now-dirty hands, gently fill
the pot with your compost, making space for the root ball so it
isn't squished. Put the Rubber Plant back in and then pat more
compost around the roots and up to the root collar. You can add
a few tablespoons of worm compost to the very top: it's high-
test food for all plants! Now, fill a jar with water. Pour a little
water on top so that the new soil runs down into the roots and
makes contact with them and there are no air pockets. Maybe
you have to add a bit more worm poo to level it up again to the
root collar. Then, put one hand over the soil and pour water onto
your hand so that the compost castings run down into the pot.
You are watering the plant and washing your hand (well, the first
washing) at the same time.

Are you feeling any better? I am.

Like it or not, every choice we make, every thing we own, every
action we take, every thought or idea we have, and every sound
or word we utter or write or read, has ecological and political and
material and emotional webs of interconnections (the workers in
the Miracle-Gro factory who moved the box with the fertilizer you
will eventually choose to buy; the spot in the field in Costa Rica
where the Rubber Plant grew; the hungry mice in the basement
at Sean's house...). And our involvement in these webs, whether
as owners or roommates or Walmart greeters or bugs on plants,
is part of a future that goes on and on, in every direction in space
and in time, without discernible end.

The unhealthy Rubber Plant, and the table where it sits, and the kitchen that holds the table are not just things. And we're not independent beings acting freely on the world of those things. Our relations to words and objects (and thus to ourselves) are not disconnected blips in space and time: A feeling here. A trademark there (Tomcat Blue Maxx). A leaf dropping there. A humming along to the radio in the store. A text from Bell. A feeling of annoyance. A debit card making the right sound on the tap. A plastic bag in a plastic bag.

It all hangs together as a moving, living sort of thereness. This thereness is what living is, what it does. And it will continue to do that, to be there, no matter what. Whether Sean is clinically depressed or joyous or neutral about his plant or himself being alive; whether you feel depressed or joyous or neutral as this story is told to you; whether you write a poem about this feeling or not, none of it will change the thereness of what is.

But because we participate in the shifting pattern of living thereness, it can be changed, and in fact is already always changed by us. By each choice. Yes, even something so "insignificant" as binning a houseplant with brown saggy leaves. Each word. Yes, even the word "hope". Each series of words—arranged as a syllogism or a poem or talking in bed—bends the thereness of our lives, of the lives we are trying to live, one way or another. And so, it bends those of any other being who is part of our web.

Dear Patient Reader, poet and lover of poetry, lover of the Earth, depressed person, person who is concerned with depression and climate change: Here's the punchline.

a) We humans have unique capacities particular to each of us: sensitivity, carefulness, imagination, logic, attentiveness, giant squid-like tentacles of intelligence, capacity to love, memory, absurdity, empathy, skills in listening and seeing, discernment of beauty, despair, touch, melody, rhythm, smell, noticing, caring, hating. Ee all use or deploy some or all of these, all the time, to some degree.

b) And we can develop them. All of them. The nice ones and the not nice ones. When we have worked, with intention, and with good coaches or teachers (you need many and varied teachers), and whatever else we might use (a poem?) to get better at these latent talents, two new capacities emerge:

i) The ability to sense the shifting difference between one situation and the next... and sometimes even the next... But not like chess moves. It's not linear. It's the entire ecology of reality as we participate in it directly as the pieces and the player and the board. So, the sensing we're doing is entirely from the inside, so to speak. But we can become very good at this. Or not. It depends.

ii) And, the ability to judge one situation as better or worse than the one before, and the one after that, using that sensitivity and from that involvement. That's ethics. That's political. That's also what we can do. And, for better or worse, that's realistically, truly, no-bullshit hubris and false hope, all we can do.

So, me and that guy Sean who texted me about his houseplant, and the soil, and the worms, and the plastic, and you, and these words you're reading, and the truckdrivers and cardboard boxes, and your mental health as you read, and that field in Costa Rica, we're all co-participants. We are a permanent ongoing part of the thereness as it happens. And at the same time, we are active participants in it. All the time and everywhere. In every present. In every future. Yes, the future of the Rubber Plant. And the future of the planet. And the future of ourselves.

Your sick plant on the table affects you. You throw it in the garbage. How do you feel? You go to Best Buy. How do you feel? You come home from Best Buy and put the plant on the table. How do you feel? Your new plant looks nice. How do you feel? In the morning you are too depressed to get out of bed. How do you feel? The plant is not watered because you are in bed. How does it feel? How do you feel about that? Tomorrow you are still as depressed. The future is the same as the last one.

Did you hear what I just said? One little sick houseplant being noticed and responded to by us—us—is itself a living moment, a good moment. As full and as good a moment as is possible. We are responding. This is critical. This responding is just as much an event, believe it or not, as 9/11 (NYC, Chile). Or the Columbia Icefield glacier retreating to rubble. Or Greta Thunberg being arrested. Or the cure for cancer. Or my friend's son dying by suicide. It is. Believe me. It is. And it matters that we know this. It is critical that we know this. This is where we literally can and do matter. We aren't terrorists, though we are related to terrorists and terrorism in some ways. We aren't strongly part of the web that is the icefield. We aren't globally recognized activists. And we aren't dead yet from mental illness or cancer. But as we are living in our actual lives, we can feel out whether we, and things, are getting better, or worse, and shift, and shift. Or not.

So, what does all this mean for poetry in a time of climate disaster?

Is the purpose of poetry is to give meaning to the world? Nope. The world already has meaning, though poetry has a peculiar power to enter into and direct the flows of meaning, beyond just the meaning of words.

Is the purpose of poetry is to give structure in a moment of chaos? Nope. Chaos already has structure, though a poem can be part of (re)structuring the next moment of that chaos.

Is the purpose of poetry to bear witness? Sure, but what else can it participate in, productively, beyond just looking? What would those poems feel like and sound like and look like?

Is the purpose of poetry to make us attentive to the thereness in which we participate? Yes! Poems draw us close to their subject, expanding empathy and curiosity through nearness.

Might poetry help you notice and care about your houseplant, or your roommates, or your planet? Yes. Why yes, it could.

Khashayar Mohammadi
Movement XV

what are we reading really
    what moves past us
        to never catch on?
        it's ok.
        let's ask
        more than we answer
    I don't like strict rules for writing
    I don't like form and style and format
    I don't adhere to the DAFFODILS style guide
    I don't like how the vocative works in English
after all what are DAFFODILS but prescriptions
    the data shows with staggering precision
        that speech crumbles
        when non-referential

    once...
        in a past life
    I was the tribe's greatest speaker
herding sacred sheep with sacred horns
its not the streets, or the roads, or the food
or the heat, or the home, or the medicine
it's not the sex and the hospital
it's in everything and none will ever be fixed
all you wish and all you want and all you love
and all you hope and all you want and all you
wish and all that keeps you
        no.
    not here.
    another life perhaps
DAFFODILS don't grow here anymore
speech dries here on the tongue

don't run it'll all be sadness early or not
an hour and a half is a blink of an eye
     but also a lifetime
     don't worry
          nothing matters
     fall down slowly in the line

Movement XVI

that dark resignation to loss. how long to run after joy and just find construction cones scattered. I take out the trash and who knows maybe I'm resilient to pesticide. some relief comes in the form of needles. I'm defeated by numbers. It simply won't happen. it just can't be that easy, to descend and to fall. concede and retreat. I miss being firmly sat in the middle of a patch of dirt you can claw into. it's finished. all is lost. skyscrapers no longer scrape the sky. clouds have all moved out of our town. I used to write differently so speak to me NOW, through the noise my hand is piercing. you've got the right idea, sitting with coffee table magazines and tuned into classical music. the weight of sleep, the emergent shapes in the city's blight. please don't read this as somnolent resignation. I have crumbled my hopes into crumbs and fed them to the ducks. I spend my day swimming through the city's various excreta. the question forms a poem which can make a poem in the reader's response. I learn yielding from plant material, curl like the corner of the bamboo leaf under stress of exhibition. the problem with the question is that once posed, it's hard to flip the "you" and the "I".

Movement XVII

what.
is a question.

if context.
is just melting snow outside.

Jennifer Wenn

Fire and Flood

From Australia aflame to
Pakistan drowning, an apocalypse
is shaking itself awake;
whistling past a threatening graveyard
I summon a bubble of
distraction and inattention
but signs and portents
slither in through unseen fissures and
coalesce into dystopian visions:
With Mad Max and Furiosa
I tear around a post-doomsday wasteland
in desperate quest of almighty fuel,
the only real goal to
avoid being vulture food,
but any Pyrrhic desert triumph
is swept away by a nightmarish tempest,
whereupon I join Lear and his Fool
on the blasted heath,
and while the erstwhile king howls
at the gale and deluge I cower,
uselessly,
looking for a sign,
hoping for a sheltering tree
with roots deep enough to
anchor in blazing barrens,
strong enough to
defy the moor-lashing storm,
just one craggy testament of life
while I await the
Godot of tranquillity.

Ode to an 'Empty' Lot

Mike my bicycle guy
First made me look.

Seeking a non-literary path to
Reducing head noise,
Prodded by my neglected figure,
I rediscovered two-wheeled pedalling,
Found my way to Mike,
Listened, and followed his gaze:
A green gap in urban concrete
Threatened by all-conquering pavement,
Tagged as empty, but sheltering a
Precious little ecosystem
From grasses to beetles to birds,
A tiny cousin to ancient
West Coast forest sanctuaries
Proffering spiritual serenity
In the face of rapacious chainsaws.
I saw too in Mike's patch a
Mirror of my search's goal,
A precious little interlude of
Peace amidst tumult,
Fragile and fleeting but
Yearning for hope and renewal
In recollection of Limoncocha's
Once-decimated primeval jungle,
Now the domain of
Life searching within, recalling the wonder,
Life reaching out in collective resurrection
Of the memory.

The little lot was still thriving,
Last time I went by,
Sending forth optimistic seeds of rebirth,
Corporeal for its modest tract and
Perhaps further afield,
And transcendent ones taking root
In those led to pause and see.

Milkweed

Butterflies dubbed monarch,
wisps of sunrise laced with starry night,
winddancing an impossible migration;
but beauty needs a substrate: enter humble milkweed,
bleeding creamy latex when wounded,
once thriving here and there and elsewhere,
once prized for salve, life-preserver stuffing and more,
then deemed nuisance, tagged for summary extirpation;
those dependent fragile flashes of splendour fading in tandem.

Finally, straws firmly grasped, one incipient fall
six hopeful milkweeds joined my little meadow,
chicken wire protection from the dog,
botanical competition thinned.
Spring saw a return of the special lightish green,
long firm veined ovals reaching out;
alas, no flowers and no seedcases, not yet.
I hovered and tended, waited and pondered.

With a flourishing spread, subterranean rhizomes
announced unseen burrowing come second summer;
and third; and then—fragrant rosy clusters,
thrusting tumescent pods; and a few monarchs.
Late summer's yellowing became autumn brown;
several hulls opened a crack, releasing fluffy messengers
to ride the frosty breeze, but most remained clamped shut.
Winter settled in, chill blasts split some others,
many lost seedlings to fall into a frozen embrace,
lucky ones cradled by the nearby hemlock to await a better fate.
But the determined husks hung on through cold's despond
till the ordained day, only then releasing tufts
of faith and vernal renewal to waft on Nature's breath,
needful spots sought to build anew and
summon again sovereign wonders.

Amanda Shankland

Jerusalem

Just a long sleeve-shirt under your spring jacket, a toque, and
   your favorite checkered scarf from the homeland
Examining the curve of your lower lip and the way your adam's
   apple moved, you spoke,
"Remember that the amazing thing about a tree is that it is implied
   from the seed from the very beginning"
Under old leather shoes worn thin, your feet were bare
Snow covered the ground, I lay my long tweed coat down so we
   could sit
Aged well past your short years, by the weight of a thousand
   fallen grandfathers
Lamenting the mischievous mystery that tries to express itself
   through insanity
Embracing my hand in yours, lying back to look at the sky, to kiss,
   to fall into the void
My mind was tired of bearing a childhood's worth of fear, so I
   decided to let go of the burden and befriend death

Tenochtitlan

The sun god Huitzilopochtli kept darkness at bay by consuming
    the hearts of men
Energy contained in human hearts were enough to light the sky
No sacrifice was too great
Or too small
Cempasuchil flowers break the pavement
Here lies the seeds of another revolution
Taking root in the bloodied soil of fallen warriors
I am a helpless child lost in the rural market on Dia de Los Muertos
The strange faces fill my nightmares
Looking for the comfort of my lost mother
Another woman sold in the aftermath of the Alvarado massacre
Naked, cold, consumed by a darkness no longer kept at bay

Limehouse

Light shines through the white pines
I am lying in the snow looking up at the clouds
My body is covered in blood, not mine
Every sound is an echo of the people who are buried here
He built our house on ancient burial ground
Our innocent childhood laughter calmed their lost souls
Underneath my skin they found sanctuary
Souls finding refuge in my delicate, gentle frame
Exorcisms would be performed in silence

Conyer Clayton

mountaintop removal glare[1]

as we drive
in the ravine
rain pools
undrinkable
uncollected
barrels in
useless rivets
down
the twisting
roadways I keep
squinting
my neck
around
the curve of   to see
if   to a catch a glimpse of   is
that the end of   is that really an
incoming storm
or   a sunset   pollution   a quarry
what   is the use of
the definition of *natural*   when they argue
that this is also *natural*
they thicken these words
till we choke

how many clouds
does it take
to flatten
a mountaintop?
I thought
that we could
mine the heart of air
to make it solid   as if
the clouds were a pile
of gravel

tucked up between
two green mountains

as if words were

as if   bodies weren't

I thought if I kept
looking one day
I would see it
instead I put a hat on
and blinked
out the sun

[1] Mountaintop removal is a destructive coal mining practice that began in Appalachia, and remains practiced today in several states including Kentucky, where I was born and raised. It leaches toxic heavy metals into water supply, destroys the land, and can result in long-term health ramifications for the humans and non-human beings living in the surrounding areas, to name but a few of the negative effects of the practice.

human + human = ♥

　　　　　　　　　　　a storied separation
　　　　　　　　　　　the glacial mother pulled away
　　　　　　　　　　　for the boulder's own good

every year
the rocks grow
dirt marks their height
in lines
like pen marks on a door frame

assume

　　　　　　　　　　this rock has no mother

　　　so I scrub it

　　　　　　　clean　of

　　　　　　　　　　spray-painted　　♥s

my pants now
blemished
stained with self-love

I ask my co-worker

Were you near the window? Did you see the wind turn sideways?
The weather has insomnia. It's tossing and turning and taking
trees to sleep with it. If the clouds can't rest, neither will the walls.
The weather grumbles to itself and then storms through the door.
Deep breathing, ushering the kids away from the windows, I tell
myself again: my next job will be easier on my body, the next
generation will do better. But even as I huddle against the most
structurally sound wall in the arena as the wind threatens to the
rip the roof off, I can't help but empathize with the storm. Climate
change the chronic pain of earth's overworking. I shake the
doorknob to the janitor's closet but it's locked. I blame capitalism
for at least 50% of my muscle tension and the majority of this
derecho. Can we just put a pin in all of this? How many times a
day does nature need to stretch? 3 x 30 seconds? Should I set an
alarm? The sun doesn't have the body awareness to align into
proper posture. When the whole world is burned out, a single
lightning bolt is the least of our worries. I come home and double-
check all my insurance plans. My house, my car, my body. What
about the world? Who is insuring that?

Maryam Gowralli

When Finding a Lover in the Anthropocene

Sweetheart, know that the romance never dies,
it comes to a head in the face of disaster
moving through description, depression
and the realization we are living in a
terribly translated world.

      Sayang,[1] to love correctly means
      to understand the Anthropocene,
      what it means to live in an ecosphere,
      I touch you desperately through a wasting climate, reclaiming
          my mother tongue—
          healing through
      the ethics of indigenous languages, mitochondrial bodies
      and cosmologies with no tenses
                [as my arms rest] [rested] [will rest]
      on your thighs, while wildfires
                [burn] [burned] [will burn].

Sweetheart, my language helps us understand,
how temporal orthodoxy in a wasteland
fucked us up—we will never be completely aware
of how time
          [passes] [passed] [will continue to pass]
and in what contexts our lovemaking traverses onto.
But with maddening wisdoms, lapping tongues and languages tell us—
          [what they contribute] [contributed] [are fully flung
          into]
          [future contributing]
impacts which shake organisms:
humans, wildlife and otherwise.

Sayang, the sound of your orgasm signifies the limbs
            [entangling] [entangled] [leading to
            impending entanglements],
a climax of comprehension—now
            [we return] [returned] [will always be
            returning to]
the remembrance of what was once previously submerged
by colonial hands: mountains providing guidance and wise-
      cracking trees.

Sweetheart, know that the romance never dies,
like our touch exemplifying existence
            [we take accountability] [have taken
            responsibility]
            [will take the more-than-human ethos future-
            tense]
shivering microbial bodies, a displaced language, and a
      traumatized world
            [constantly evolving] [long since evolved] [to
            forever evolve].

[1] 'Sayang' is 'Darling' in Bahasa Indonesia.

17

Reel Headaches

///

a flicker into black, they told me not to watch with the dogs, the
children, the adults, and bacteria. that was fine enough. but what
was i supposed to do when my brain told my heart, my liver, and
my kidneys that i couldn't go outside that i had to be cramped in
here? a furiously heart-broken robot, suffering from soft tissue, the
nostalgia of rubbing shoulders, and a headache. there is nothing
but scopophilia here, stuck in social media la la land, doom-
scrolling: news of a disappearing snail, earthquakes ad infinitum,
empty anagrams to reconciliation, AI generators stealing art scenes
once mine, and crypto-boys claiming to be shadow-banned by
technocratic websites. quicksand, i find myself in a digital hellscape,
an indicator species of the times, sinking

///

static as cracked pepper, tongue in flashback. if only i could
pull the pixels and spice my food, starlight condiments for my
culinary skills. But instead, a month's worth of groceries morph,
a symbol: economic dislocation and the need for a sturdier tote
bag. i see myself on the precipice of food deserts and dunes—are
there any food centres here? but even the plants feel pain? are
the interest rates and takeout boxes worth it? we can't help it if
a TV show seeds consciousness, capitalism telling citizens of too
many breaching gates. zombie hordes: environmental refugees

and asylum-seekers ready to chomp and eat my bones, blood for ketchup. here comes a downward spiral of consumption and nation-building, a box inserts the images in and out of conflicting ideologies, i we they need to eat too

///

thoughts amid binge-watching and soundtracks: even the most neurotypical sees the universe in fragments, an existence of consciousness, normal as ever. but i we they can no longer postpone sustainable projects, calls for texture and symbiosis in climate resistance. the fungus finds me, in between the cracks and pulls a network, meshing skeletons with synthetic chips and a fast-spreading colony—the triage is a homecoming, the hemorrhaging of skulls transforming into fertile frolicking fusions in the badlands. with empty stomachs and a carbon footprint, we wave to the Swamp Thing, the Body Snatchers and Cordyceps from *The Last of Us*, passing hellos. Sipping on mushrooms, kernels of selfsame pain, pop an Advil and say: did you know that happiness comes best now that we're all earth moon-signs in a dead world?

Sydney Hegele
/ psychodiagnostic assessment report /

My father and I used to walk on water in winter / *traumatic experiences starting in childhood* / he said the ice was thick and safe on our side of the lake from pumphouse park / *police called to the house frequently* / a blur of white where concrete ended and abyss began / *instances when they feared for their life and wellbeing* / summer kids cannonballed into algae nets more slime than wet / *lacking sufficient guidance on adaptive emotion modulation strategies* / filaments thin like loose thread, caught on rocks / *engaged in dissociation as a way of managing and escaping highly distressing emotions* / SWIM AT OWN RISK / *fully developed "characters"* / January ice turned undertow to tundra / *each character has their own unique name, voice, age, gender, and personality* / hardened snow, piled and pointed like mountain peaks / *insufficient emotional and physical safety impacted their trust in others* / I was not afraid / *particularly men* / to die, then / *flashbacks* / but I am now / *anhedonia* / I have not seen Lake Ontario frozen since I was ten / *frequent nightmares and night terrors* / warmer winters make ice sheets brittle and slick / *auditory and aromatic triggers* / how much is too much weight to hold? / *hyperarousal* / I am older. I have seen safety disappear / *avoidance of reminders of the traumatic events* / there are two lakes here this year / *frequent experiences of depersonalization and derealization* / reality's rising tide / *DSM-5 diagnostic criteria are met for dissociative identity disorder* / and the memory of those winters, alive in the body / *complex post-traumatic stress disorder* / my father taught me to survive a fall through thin ice / *emotional dysregulation; negative self-beliefs; interpersonal difficulties* / you must exhale underwater / *started after the sexual assault* / and follow the direction of the bubbles / *highly negative view of themselves* / to the frozen surface / *extreme distress* / so that you can break through / *has several strengths* / but you cannot fall / *supportive partner* / if you do not walk / *success in their writing* / and you cannot fall / *desire to understand* / if there is no ice / *despite enduring* / the heat is my fault / *they likely internalized* / I miss winter / *criticism* / I am better / *enduring* / we are water / *enduring* / frozen / *enduring* / thawing / *enduring*

Gary Barwin & Elee Kraljii Gardiner

Riven Museum[1]

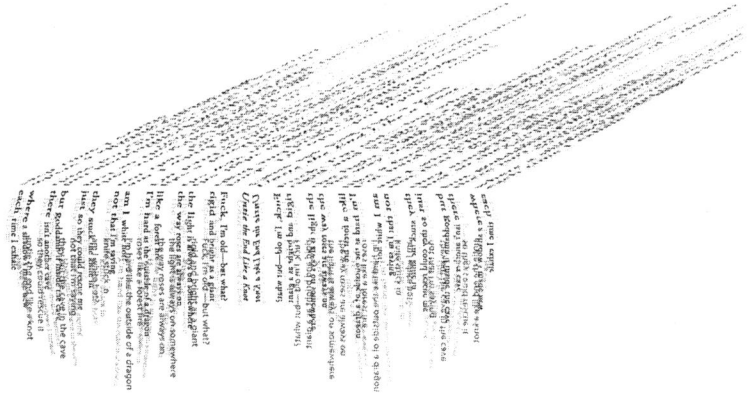

[1] From *Watcher* (Timglaset Press).

Odobenus rosmarus (grief)

heavy gut sun soaker
floe loafer
forlorn tusker
lamp throater
intimate bellower
dusk crasher
bone whiskered drone striker
ice sorrower
fracturer
keener
boxer of night
      of day
fragile visitor

In a boat; keening

it's not
    I'm not

    waves

without

        without

Riven Museum

days collapse in snowfall blue as sleep
rebellion teaches the clock

at the centre of the icicle
an hour by another name

"later" is a door warm at the hinge
yesterday is its own mirror, gold as gold

rivers become a map unfurled under afternoon sun
a clock a shortcut as the crow flies

dusk times grief
or distance plus dawn
our faces refracted by meltwater

The Eye You See

                    something about rain
runs like the rim of sugar around the glass
of my eye

history raises a hand for help

a handful of birds in a bath of milk
hope a century wide
            a squinty poison

the distance of my own looking
            on fire here
                    also here

gregor Y kennedy

Anxiety

the eating of flesh by parasites
by Paradise
by parachutes not packed right

the failure of brakes
of Fates
of lakes
of being born too late

the conflicted death of wealth
of health
of attachments to a grounded self

going going gone
coming coming soon
every dream a choking nightmare
in this burning locked bedroom

to our children
to our youth
to our nervous system
& our IQs
what on earth
      Poor Earth!
does it all do?

i'm so scared i want to die
stick a threaded needle in my eye
that makes me blind & makes me cry
& saves me from the ugly question "why?"

bipolar

bipolar
warming
both ends
burning
    globular candle
    big ball of wax
    midnight oil
spill overshadows
waters icy
their cold edge
knocked off
glaciers floating
on the rocks
whiskey ocean
fearfully drunk
tundra fiery
methane mounting
serotonin leaking
depression
elation
scared as Hell
on Earth
bipolar
sympathy
climatic
solidarity
feeling the planet
feel
natural reaction
to extreme destruction
both ends
burning
up and down
what comes around

goes straight
into the mind
thought lost
but really
it's just accurately
registering.

Too Hot

the heat is on
your head on
your shoulders
keep it there—
your head not the heat—
keep it cool
but not cut off
from the burning tears
flowing upward
from your heart
shut off
because its sensors sensed
TOO HOT!
and did its self-preserving job
of fighting burnout
with frost-cold flight

your head cut off
      too hot!
a Death Valley deadly desert
below the sea level
of your water body
whose tides tell wind and rain
how to play their games

madness
is all the rage
everyone to some degree
pushing up the mercury
until it cracks
the narrow hollow glass
slow down this quicksilver
please
but do not touch the golden race

Prayer in the Age of Climate Change

All will be well
Warbles the nuthatch from Norwich
In bird language
We don't understand.
We burned its dictionaries
To roast our chickens.

Palms together
Hands wringing
As much as these bells
Of alarm
With their big ball tongues
Cut out to make damn sure
Nobody's denied the right
Of sleeping.

Fear is old and tired
It tells the same demented stories
ad iram
We get angry
Don't listen
Nothing to do
With us.

There's a dream
Called forgiveness
It haunts us in the mourning
Like the dove's heartbreak cooing
If we believe we had it
We might journal our way back
To remembrance.

The glass ceiling.
The concrete floor.
A sense of nowhere to go
Much less of home.

Yet I know a certain patch of trilliums
On the brink of blooming
Who gesture with three green hands
A universal sign of hope.

So true.
And equally
Not far away
The forest fires
Have never raged so wild
So early.

Aaron Kreuter
Bad Mood Rising

It's a truth at least as old as the limbic cortex: that bad mood is on its way. A feeling you must learn to recognize each of its four thousand times. The bad mood lifting. The bad mood descending. (Bad mood rising; bad mood smizing.) Yes, I may be full of the bad juice, but guess what? So are you. Knock knock. Who's there? Your chemical imbalance. And it's got home invasion on its mind. (Three Day Bad Mood—still zero calories, but now with even more self loathing!) In my teenage years, oh in my teenage years. The only difference between a bad mood at 280 ppm, 420 ppm, 1062 ppm? The weight of the stars on our pleading lungs, you useless bilaterian. (At what ppm do the bad moods cease you type into your dictaphone, whose batteries are long dead.) Time to stand by the window. Time for a cold compress. Time to pick a new mantra. Is this the world my inaction has built? Sheet, weighted, duvet, quilt.

Good Mood Fleeting

Quilt, duvet, weighted, sheet. It is possible to be in a good mood under all that blanketage, post-coital say, or with a derivative post-apocalyptic novel, but why not venture out into the world with your flat-earth heart and heat-death soul? Just peel back the layers like a toy onion (as the old song goes: the walrus is... extinct), find the hard crunchy serotonin centre. The pill kills the wet dreams, you discover, among other things. Surprisingly, you miss it: the thrill of waking into golden revelation before another morning of coffee and dread. At first, the bad moods are, well, still there. You spend too much time on Cheese Grater, playing confirmation bias with the therapy bots. Sometimes (the bots say) you have to let the moods pass through you, an electric current. Sometimes (they intone) you have to search frantically for the outlet. Sometimes, you have to drive six hours to the waterfall. Sometimes, you have to force yourself into the rocky bowl of cold water. And then, like an orange shock over green dunes, it's gone. Driving into the sun, the air conditioning on.

Concetta Principe
The Painting of How I Feel

Sunflowers, smelling in strokes that washed Van Gogh's mind, drove him into a mad universe. Van Gogh drank the Kool-Aid, so to speak. He filled his jug with madness. The texture of what he drank bordered with small white flowers was this scarf I had once. I branded my neck with this silk of madness.

But when you've got a jug of people running all around. A jug a jug a jug a jig a jug. I see Matisse's women dancing. Imagine their rhyme on the yellow spectrum. A jig of order of alder of willow branches. Cracked.

The crack through Van Gogh's canvas. Sunlight sprouting from the jug and everything smells of cut grass, the gas of the lawn mower. A dancing thigh, painted over. So many things to fracture. Eggs, their yolk. Walls of Perkin's wallpaper. Walnuts. The mystery. Madly, I stuff Christie with the scent of silver catkins. No green left at this hour of the year.

Of lemon. It cracks the mystery of cosmic disability. It cures scurvy. It hurts. It is a bad Saab, meringue pie, a bruise on the seam of a day. It is pus and puckered lips, purple fade. And Biscotti, spiced with this fade is good.

But above all, there's Picasso's blue. It is the ground I walk on, holding madness shining brightly. It is the jug, folding cosmic grass into itself. It is the wide crack and soft willow smelling silver. Feeling this blue, period.

AJ Dolman
Contamination

1st.
Quantum theory explains almost everything
is hidden, our alternative trajectories
obscured by singularity
of focus; every brave world
an iceberg, its tip melted away

2nd.
This island was sacred
so we named the boardrooms
for what was—grasses, berries,
cedar and sedge, dense brush
that held shale in place,
water, muskrats, et cetera

3rd.
My boss jokes that I chose
the best seat in the building.
It's easy to smoke signal ideals
from a dumpster fire. Last month I
dropped my cellphone on the street,
nearly lost myself

Like scabs, we replace
the day work of seagulls,
unflappable between banks, set up
at a confluence of provinces, languages,
little rock between bridges barely
weathered by our surroundings, perpetual
churning at the base, towards ocean

4th.
Once they excavated a hundred
thousand tonnes of poisoned soil,
they deemed the land remediated,
peeled back centuries, rampant
brickworks, black birch frames, shipped
in miles of fresh rebar, built shiny,
glass nests up into the clouds

5th.
I snap a picture of the seething river below Zibi,
post it to my socials:

"Sure, the commute was a nightmare,
but the view from here is something,"
and count as my likes roll in

Complacency

Lao Tzu said to be like water;

so drunk and desperate to belong,

I leave my boots on the shore,

wade into the Crowsnest River

and evaporate

Scenery sways improbably green

and slate against air

exhausted by weathers

The wine, this glass—

wasn't I holding one?

The no swimming sign,

its bullet holes, illusion

there is no highway behind

that crest of scrub and cottonwoods

if we ignore the heavy shushing

of tires over pavement

Everything out here

is a chimera, except our intentions

and the cold rapids

searing my shins.

But only one of these thoughts

is likely true

Tara McGowan-Ross
If I had a son I would call him Ben

for Ben Prunty

When I was a child a kind farmer told me that
in the grip of disaster, it is best to loose the horses.
Well-meaning saviours arrive with their animals
mulched in the panic-box of the trailer, beaten
to death by the pursuit of freedom. Rarity makes
fear a crisis, for predators.   Prey know it

to be the fabric of the world. My best friend tells
me all life on earth shares a single common
ancestor, with a name. My therapist explains that
my obligations change as something gets closer.
Sometimes I wish I had gone with you to slaughter
pigs, when invited.   At the dairy farm,

my cousin-calf takes my whole hand in his mouth
like I have something to offer him that isn't death.
Pigs are a somewhat closer relation. I feel it when
I eat them and I change.   In the years
since you killed yourself, I have stopped eating pork
altogether. When I feed the mean thing it gets

bigger and more hungry. Perhaps to feed most
of me I must live my whole life with some small
part starving. Your best friend kissed me and I liked
it more than he did.   His last name and birthplace
are the same as my great-grandfather's so I let this
be a wedge. I could call a son Luca for *last universal*

common ancestor. Ambrose, for my great-grandfather.
But I won't have children. On that coast, my
homeland is taking on water so quickly it is nearly
time for new maps. If the people are the language
are the land, what is my body preparing to lose?
When I arrive on the other coast I am readied only

for horrors, which makes me vulnerable to the
beauty of things.   The downtown Eastside
street where my brother died is mostly full of people
who are smiling, and the number of brothers dying
appears small by comparison. The first time I saw
another Indian open a felled ruminant I anticipated

my disgust but not my desire. I leave to plant trees
which will save no one but me for as long as it takes
to plant them. During the drive I think of the white
men who arrived unprepared for how seriously the
cold takes her obligations, how they redrew some
map to make people into meat. How many babies

grow up without stories about what the mean
thing does when it's fed. Satisfied,   I consider
what to mulch next in the panic-box of the poem.
The disaster arrives all around me.   Ben,
there is more than one way to consume a person.
I tell myself you'd understand, but I don't know.

We weren't close.   When I arrive
in the burnt forest I am ashamed to find it beautiful.
Full of fire-scarred horses and their perfect children
who don't know any other way for things to be.

D.A. Lockhart

Upon Seeing the Sky Through Outstretch Mimosa Leaf

Pop-up showers
     above the mouth
   of the river.

The heat   the heat   the heat

and the chiskukus
    splashes in the koi pond.

audible solely in song.

Through spread leaves
   the clouds grow
   and slouch eastward.

towards Chatham
     towards Moraviantown
        towards distant dry fields.

Burning Off Last Season

Across Roblin, a neighbour burns last season
away. Whiteness of smoke, a fresh sign of new
pontiff, drifts low across the stilled lake surface.
Omen admires its own form before folding into
a soft dissipation of air, heat and ash, last season
sublimates into a solemnity of white, aloft, refuses
the touch of water. Fire-rendered decay softens
into cognizant medicine, and with this ceremony
a year comes undone. Ceremony shall deliver rich
black nourishment to what follows. And the lake
shall remained untouched, this passage reflected
across a stilled surface. Through stifled spring light,
I watch this unfold and consider how the ashen
brown country will find its way back to green.

Revelations about Lilacs at Roblin Lake

As if one night I awaken
to find and understand
that Bowie could be dead,
as I dance to "Life of Mars"
in the living room of a dead
poet's part-time home. Surrounded
by thoughts and lines of the end,
a dead man's library of dead men,
me dancing, air cleared with hints
of spring rain. Ruminating in four-
four time at sixty-three beats per
minute, this is elegy. This is rebirth.
With each step, a kindled awareness
that all of creation is life
and death. This is the way
words and stories and songs
take root, in elegy, in relation
to light-footed tavern moves
in this nushèmakw medicine nexus.
Outside, the first fragrant
clusters of lilac are bursting open
to greet the rain. And we know
that the heavens are as full
as the world around us is empty.
But this poem, this dance,
is a saddening bore. 'Cause
I wrote it ten times or more
and it's about to be writ again
As I ask you reckon with
how revelations arrive, lilacs
blooming in the rain, and elegies
are outpourings of awakenings
to the things we miss in between.

Conal Smiley
Mystery Ward

I suppose if I was well
but what does well mean

kerosene, matches
an ocean of fire

> *in a place like this*
> *the ward, a world*

of its own
a man prepares
dinner for his wife

I would be happy
and suppose well
with white walls and mercy

the coarse cry of oil-slicked gulls
pivoting around our doors

a couple hands out
flyers for a cause

> *but I'm happy if also unhappy*

tape hiss in forests
stretching down corridors

and happiness
doesn't come well
with shoelaces undone

to catch a minnow in the hand
since the salmon have fled

it's very clear our bodies
are here to stay

and ripped out of shoes
flapping against linoleum

I lean against the inviting moss
climbing the ward walls

a young boy gets a haircut
he is happy with
so there are no hazards

but I suppose I'm well
if it means I'm in this place of unwell

but what are the hazards
the afternoon wanes into evening

a trash can on fire
a ballpoint pen and
belt given up on admission

when hazards are only warnings
unhappiness is a placemat

air surrounds the body
like a glove, tightening

and warnings aren't
to be ignored

for all types of dishes to sit on
unless they are ignored by most
horizons stripped of trees

but to be well is a dish
that I'm

    not I am or am not I

boarding up the ward
for worse weather
sitting on a placemat

They will keep building cities
with hazards in place or not

until they all merge together
whatever the matter may be

    like the interlocking
    fingers of two hands

In Blue

a flood   our demise

backwards backwoods through
blue

rooms   they kept us

silent in   at nights

when silence and somnolence
copulate in blue

we lost
the record

of where to end

a flood for the ages an end
for our time

in fantasy a proposition
to hold through blue nights

when the surf was high

fear tight in our lips

Nina Jane Drystek
nest

gather as many blankets as you can find & one a clean bedsheet
gather a pen & some pieces of loose paper
clear a space on the floor, set aside the bedsheet, pen & paper
make a nest with the blankets you gathered, add some pillows if
    you like
as you build remember a moment of tenderness
between you & a lover
between you & a friend
between you & someone you consider a parent or guide
when you are done building the nest, stand over it & look in
what images do you see in the contours of the folds?
is there a pattern?
pick up your pen & write or draw what you see on your skin

pick up the loose sheets of paper, scrunch them up & toss them
    into the nest
pick up the bed sheet, shake it out & find the edges of two corners
pull it around you like a cloak & walk twice around the nest
stop. pull the sheet up over your head & settle in like it's your bed
lie still
listen to the nest, to the room beyond
listen to the beyond rooms & beyond worlds
listen to the sheets
remember the worst thing you have ever tasted & hold the taste
    in your mouth
how does it make your body feel?
slowly begin to emerge, feel around the outside of the nest for
    the pen
take some crumpled paper out from under you
scrunch & hold everything together for a moment
take a breath
smooth out the paper & imagine you are the guardian of your
    enemy
write observations & advice for them along the creases in the page
drawn on the ideas the nest showed you

when creases collide write words overtop of each other

when you are done read it aloud then fold it up into the tiniest
    triangle possible
leave it by your bed
open it when you are having a bad day

Kathryn Mockler
Pareidolia

The ability to see faces in inanimate objects is called pareidolia. Scientists used to think if you had this proclivity, you had a form of psychosis, but now they think you might be neurotic, happy, or normal, which is just another way of saying shit happens.

In this picture of the sky there are two clouds. One of the clouds looks like a man with his hand on his hip and the other cloud appears as a giant head with no body.

The man and the head are arguing about the existence of God, climate change, and whether the gains are worth the losses when it comes to extinction.

The man is an atheist, the sort of person involved in his local men's movement which, to his disappointment, has turned out to be a bunch of middle-aged men bitching about their wives. Unfortunately, the man is not married and never has been, so he's often left out of the conversation.

The giant head with no body is not only declaring her belief in God, but also is claiming she is God because how else could she explain her predicament of being all head and no body. I think therefore I am God is a phrase she thought she saw on a bumper sticker when she drove through the mountains on the way to the wellness retreat.

The argument is not going very well.

Neither the man with his hand on his hip nor the giant head can manage to convince the other of their position.

And the problem with them, and with everyone else for that matter, is that they're going to stay up there in the sky bickering— neither budging on their points, neither coming up with new or interesting rhetorical strategies.

They're not going to look at the situation from the other person's point of view. They're not going to even try to understand. And why should they? They both think they're right.

So the plan for now is to just keep the fight going until one or both of them disappear.

If It Keeps Me Calm

You can't live in fear—even if what you fear is based in reality. Even if your fear is adaptive, a healthy response to a clear and present danger. If I don't like what the scientists report, I'm just going to stomp my feet and say, "Not so!"

If I feel even a little bit scared (a completely rational emotion in the face of an existential threat) I'm going to cook up a story that makes me feel better about the state of things.

It feels so good to make up these stories that I hardly ever think about who benefits from my denial or who suffers. Certainly not the people I love. And if people I love don't suffer, then that means no one suffers because I only believe in what I can see with my eyes. And if something awful befalls someone I happen to know, I'll just look for reasons to blame them for their own tough luck— maybe they didn't work hard enough or maybe what they're telling me is just all in their head.

If it keeps me calm, then that's a good thing. If I'm calm that means, I'll just get up each day with little complaint and go to work. I won't even worry that the hoarders of wealth are making everyone work more for less.

Somebody's got to be a billionaire. It doesn't have to be me as long as I have enough money. Why should I worry about things that are out of my control when they mostly affect other people? And even if they affect me too, well, what can I say but, so what?

If I thought about how every little thing I buy and consume harms another person and contributes to mass death, inequity, and the degradation of the planet, I wouldn't be able to sleep at night. And I really do need to get a good night's sleep. To be honest, most nights I sleep pretty damn well.

And if we are really watching the slow fall of civilization or the end of life on Earth—instead of feeling bad about it, I'll just consider myself lucky for getting a front row seat.

A Certain Type of Furniture

—Today I feel hopeless.

—Has anyone likened you to anything? An animal or perhaps a certain type of furniture?

—Some have said I bear a striking resemblance to a foot stool though it doesn't do wonders for the self-esteem to be likened to a foot stool. I prefer to be likened to a plant—especially one that can survive climate catastrophe.

—How does one find joy in an extinction event anyway?

—Denial.

—Is denial adaptive behaviour or maladaptive behaviour?

—A little of both.

—What kind of plant do you think I'm like?

—Moss.

—Moss is beautiful.

Karen Houle
Paimpont-Brocéliand National Forest

Thirty-seven graduate students and three faculty take a tour of the Paimpont-Brocéliand National Forest with the Forestry Technican Johnattan Barbier[1] of the National Forests Office (ONF-France) on May 29th, 2023

A yellow warbler whistled: *poooo-eeee poooo-eeeee.*
A sunlight so strong it could crush us.
Massive trees with low branches have no commercial value, zero.

We only spotted her when she moved from one branch to another
Through the big leafy oaks inundated with light,
the light that makes the fuzz of the beech leaves stand out: green shadow puppets.

I had no idea that pear trees grew in a forest.
A pear tree!

Its shiny heart leaves laughing & waving at us all along its burned branches
living branches burned from no water makes a purple that is almost black.

A strange item, that-

There are items that allow one to determine, at a distance,
the value of a life by the thickness of its trunk.
She stayed on that branch for a whole minute singing us both her songs, both of them.

A tetragnatha was carrying her eggs between her legs, crossing a leaf.
Two tree trunks had fused to form a cross at eye level.
She was especially gorgeous, with her crazy green, her zillion eyes, and her speed.

One holds the metal chain at eye level.
The U-shaped metal scope is held at arm's length.

Two or four hands are needed
To make the marks that are made on trees

For each tool in his Forestry Technician trunk: a giant ruler capable of unfolding
To 5 metres high, a rigid unpolished tongue that protected his fingers from tendonitis
when he deploys the paint bombs: a patented hammer that could not be shown to the public.

I pulled out a blade of long grass to keep my hands occupied while he talked.
I love pulling out blades of grass. I love the sensation of chopping them into small, even-sized bits with my thumbnail until my hands have lost interest. Soft and hard at the same time.

A trunk that spills out of the U-scope is a category #1: Highly Cuttable.
A trunk precisely the size of the edges of the metal U

Earns a score of zero.

How strange to use binoculars to spy on plants instead of animals. Ikea has sponsored
the observation platform for the observation of an ancient: *hoooooww old? hoooooww old?* There is a perfect tool for coring out its heart so we could know: we know

to know is to count. And while we are counting, *one-two-three one-two-three one-two-three*
we are spilling bacteria, single file, down the well-marked trail that leads right into the heart
of the forest, the heart of a very tired tree.

I have visited the old ones many times before but each time I spend an afternoon with them,
with their gigantic branches, a calm and wise power comes over me.

Commercially useless trees
are kept for the purposes of biodiversity.

And learning.

I learned how to manage a forest.
I learned State Forests are managed for people.
I learned State Forests belong to the State.

Sanctioned squares are cut out of the forest like pie dough, the rear low wall
of pine is flooded with burning daylight: blind babies immediately began pushing up & out.
If it's too dry up in the canopy, a tree will push out many new ones from her wet thick base.

In the perfect square right beside it, all the experimental little ones were smaller, stunted,
their outline sat well inside the metal U: too young to be chopped down.

One of them was only

8 km long by 2 m high surrounded by a 15 x 15 zinc mesh. Young deer can jump through that hole, big ones can clear the canopy.
The forestry agent had seen that, fleeing from a hunter.
In his canvas bag, he carried the skull and horns of a young deer.

Stitches sew together the skull of a young deer: tight curves interlace, making pine tree shapes on bone. Did you notice the long, pointy leaves of the chestnut family the same shape as the human hand? Maybe hunting with dogs is less awful than we thought.

I found the tiniest pinecone ever.
It made a perfect projectile.

Nor did my fingers expect deer horns to be so smooth.

A forest is not a number of girdled trees in a row adding up to zero: it is the wild part.
It is the wild part that leaps into a crown, the entanglement, the living lace of randomness
tatted tight and whole, a whole that lives without having to touch or name the other

every single tree grew up learning the gentlest of lean toward its neighbours: a forest
is the pressure of air that comes before the touch, a forest is the pressure of air
that looks before it asks: as I was twisting a blade of grass around my finger like a ring

I knew I simply did not understand what it feels like to agree to not to be touched after having been manhandled, and still build a universe together, way up top like that.

Coming back to the research station, the happy private gurgling of the swallows delighted me.

The foresters spoke the French of southern Brittany. A twisty French by ear.
Together they agreed to change the names of trees. They changed the names of trees
so they could shout to one across the distance
getting the work of forest management done.

"Oaks" were sung out: *chenoooo... chenooooo...*
"Beech" were sung out: *fayarrrrd... fayaaaarrrd...*

One sung out with his throat and tongue air when he came upon
a marked tree:
the other used his hand and a pen to write a series of marks down
on a dead one

On paper, that, when said out loud into air by another throat,
would be a different song, still.

The words were written in a line of ants walking single-file: the
pages are filed
at the back of the oldest book on record, made of tree flesh and
animal skin and plant stains. Inside the skin of that book, one can
always find—written down, or heard, or remembered-

the ordonnance of eternal forests:
a single yellowed warbling note that calls out—

maybe not to us,
maybe never again for us,
& maybe not even the same music
the forest sings its children with—

but she called out to us, she did, when we first arrived home:
poooo-eeee poooo-eeeee.

[1] https://www.onf.fr/onf/recherche?user_search=Johnattan+Barbier

against windshields, the necks of birds, the spokes of umbrellas

and then plummet into the whims of stone to listen, briefly

for the heavens, is to listen like rain

from the purpled hue of cloud what would it mean to listen

an inlet, a river, bent toward an ocean's mouth—
the slope of a hill, the pull of gravity into a familiar rush—like
rainwater searching for direction

without this fear of forgetting this loyalty to soil
what sort of animal would I be

what if I made myself the sky, my mind its stars to say here, worm
huddle close, lock me in
small rooms of wind

the animal I am now
speaks spring like a bird,
says only *berries, nest, twig, flight*

my right foot savours the earth's pulse knows
this body will forget everything it has touched,
is afraid to be alone

I want to trade my eyes

I want the stillness of forests, suppleness of moss a sparrow
nosing shrubs

grow something green from the trail I leave in dirt

furnish a nest from my broken eyelashes the husk of a footpath

for an osprey's eyes
fill my mouth with the feather and gristle of wings change my
breath, mistrust human speech

rain passes like spilled seeds through my hair burning holes into
the night

I want to breathe among the poplars, coax their dark trunks lance
a finger toward the moon

a billion insatiable questions.

Fiona Tinwei Lam

Three Senryu

i

BC wildfire haze
blends with contrails: Maui-bound
vacationers doze.

ii

They refuse to see—
World blind to oblivion.
Smoke must be too thick.

iii

Until the end, we
will keep pretending we're not
marching for nothing.

Dominik Parisien

Failed ode to an unknown tree?

A poem seems a poor apology.
I began, *somewhere you make breath*
possible, only I remembered
death. One moment I saw you splendid
in the sun, then every line became
a chainsaw's bucking teeth.
Can I claim I ever really cared
if I hope to see your poem on a page?
And yet here are words.
And here a few more, seeded, maybe
like you, to make breath
possible.

Brandon Wint

Whatever Splits a Raindrop
into Fourteen Splattered Gemstones

yes
voices and water say *ever, ever* where the moon says *remember me?*

its own kind of listening: a call and response always tugged toward the moon's sirening, which is restlessness, as seas are never quiet, never still—

the memory of seas, oceans full of drownings gather into my still-human ear

as unknown destinations relent to fluid—to listen like water

Grace

Small Talk

How do you tell someone
is from Vancouver?

We're always talking
about the rain.

Not the rhythm of it
as it falls

or how it smells
like an E-flat, warm

on a summer night.
Just something ordinary, like

That's some rain we're having, or
It's been a while

since we had rain.
The type of small talk

where all you have to do
is say what you see

day after day
instead of looking for the end

of the world
in every drop of rain.

Be Water

I've been trying
   not to think
about the future because
   I want to live
where we love
   the rain
like we know
   the meaning
of thirst

   Bruce Lee said to be
water—that he understood
   the power of water
when he struck it
   and it didn't suffer

I am trying
   to be water
it should be easy
   after all
on a good day
   humans are 75% water

on a bad day
   I am a drought
mouth full of sand
   nothing left to give

I remember my parents
   taping up our windows
during a monsoon
   that day
the water struck us
   like it'd suffered

every summer now
    the forest fires
    the forest fires
    the forest fires

maybe water is like us—
    it suffers in secret
ways

in my language, water's character
    is a radical: 氵[1]
there is no living 活
    no clarity 清
        no romance 浪漫
without water

    every summer now
the sprinklers bleed
    water for hours and hours
under an orange sky

    in another life
the earth doesn't know
    the meaning of thirst
and we gather
    and celebrate
a downpour
    of applause

[1] "Be Water" borrows the idea of highlighting Chinese characters with the water radical from Lydia Kwa's "Water."

About the Authors

Khashayar "Kess" Mohammadi (they/them) is a queer, Iranian born, Toronto-based poet, writer and translator. They are the winner of the 2021 Vallum Poetry Prize and the author of many chapbooks and three full-length poetry collections.

Jennifer Wenn is a trans-identified writer and speaker from London, Ontario, Canada. Her first poetry chapbook, *A Song of Milestones*, was published by Harmonia Press. Her first full-length collection, *Hear Through the Silence*, was published by Cyberwit. Coming spring 2025 from Wet Ink Books is her second collection, *Emergence*. She has also written *From Adversity to Accomplishment* (a family and social history) and has published poetry in numerous journals and anthologies. She is also the proud parent of two adult children. Visit her website at https://jenniferwennpoet.wixsite.com/home.

Amanda Shankland, Ph.D. is a writer and educator specializing in water policy, agroecology, and food systems. She earned her Ph.D. in political science from Carleton University and is currently a post-doctoral research fellow at the Global Center for Climate Change and Transboundary Waters. Her work explores the intersections of environmental justice, water policy, and community resilience. Her recent book, *Cultivating Community*, explores the politics of water management in Australian agriculture. She is also a creative writer, poet, and mother of three teenage sons.

Conyer Clayton is an award-winning writer and editor from Kentucky now living in Ottawa, whose multi-genre work often explores grief, disability, addiction, and gender-based violence through a surrealist lens. Their latest book is *But the sun, and the ships, and the fish, and the waves.* (Winner of the Archibald Lampman Award, Anvil Press). They are a Senior Editor at Augur and a member of VII, an Ottawa-based poetry collective.

Maryam Gowralli lives on Treaty 7 Territory and draws inspiration from her Trinidadian-Indian and Indonesian heritage. She is the Creative Nonfiction Editor for *filling Station* and is pursuing an MA in English Literature at the University of Calgary. Find her works at *PRISM International, Freefall, The Selkie, The Canadian League of Poets, The Caribbean Writer*, and other journals.

Sydney Hegele is the author of *Bird Suit* (Invisible Publishing 2024) and *The Pump* (Invisible Publishing 2021), winner of the 2022 ReLit Literary Award for Short Fiction and a finalist for the 2022 Trillium Book Award. Their essays have appeared in *Catapult, Electric Literature, EVENT,* and others. Their essay collection *Bad Kids* is forthcoming with Invisible in fall 2025. They live with their husband and French Bulldog in Toronto, Ontario.

Gary Barwin is a writer, multimedia artist and musician and the author of *Scandal at the Alphorn Factory: New and Selected Short Fiction 2024-1984, Ovaryman* (a play written with Tom Prime in Dead Code and other dramatic entertainments) and *Muttertongue: What is a Word in Utter Space* (with Lillian Allen and Gregory Betts), issued as an LP and a book. His work has been performed, exhibited, published and broadcast internationally. He lives in Hamilton, Ontario. garybarwin.com.

Elee Kraljii Gardiner is the author of two books of poetry, *Trauma Head* and *serpentine loop*, and editor of the anthologies *Against Death: 35 Essays on Living* and *V6A: Writing from Vancouver's Downtown Eastside*. A frequent collaborator, Elee is currently collaborating with nature via a series of durational installations that investigate the law of thermodynamics and cultural ideas regarding the passing of time. Originally from Boston, Elee directs Vancouver Manuscript Intensive, a program pairing authors with mentors. In January 2025 she became poet laureate of the City of Vancouver for three years. eleekg.com

gregor Y kennedy is a poet and retreat facilitator living and working at the Ignatius Jesuit Centre, Guelph, Ontario. Both his retreats and his writing explore the confluence of ecology and spirituality. His latest books are three volumes of poetry entitled *Reupholstered Psalms* (Novalis Press).

Aaron Kreuter is the author of two poetry collections, two short fiction collections, and an academic monograph. His 2022 poetry collection, *Shifting Baseline Syndrome*, was a finalist for a Governor General's Literary Award, was on the Raymond Souster Award for Poetry shortlist, and was included on the CBC Best Poetry Books of 2022 list. *Lake Burntshore*, a novel set at a Jewish sleepover camp, is forthcoming from ECW Press. He lives in Toronto and teaches at Trent University.

Concetta Principe is an award-winning writer of poetry, creative non-fiction, short fiction, as well as scholarship that focuses on trauma literature. Her recent project, a collection of poems on the subject of Borderline Personality Disorder, titled *Disorder* (2024), has come out with Gordon Hill Press. *Interference* (1999) with Guernica Editions, won the Bressani Award for poetry in 2000. *This Real*, published by Pedlar Press, was long-listed for the Raymond Souster Award in 2017. She teaches at Trent University.

AJ Dolman's (they/she) debut poetry book is *Crazy / Mad* (Gordon Hill Press 2024). They previously authored *Lost Enough: A collection of short stories*, and three poetry chapbooks, and has co-edited *Motherhood in Precarious Times*. Dolman's writing has also appeared in numerous magazines and anthologies. A bi/pan+ rights advocate and founder of Bi+ Canada, they live on unceded, unsurrendered Anishinaabe Algonquin territory.

Tara McGowan-Ross is an urban Mi'kmaq writer and a multi-disciplinary artist. She is the author of three books, including the Hilary Weston finalist, *Nothing Will Be Different*. Her work has been featured in print, online, and in anthologies, including *Best Canadian Poetry* and *Anthologie de la poésie actuelle des femmes au Québec*. She lives in Montreal.

D.A. Lockhart is the author of multiple collections of poetry and short fiction. His work has been shortlisted for the Trillium Book Award, Raymond Souster Award, Indiana Author's Awards, First Nations Communities READ Award, and has been a finalist for the ReLit Award. His work has appeared widely throughout Turtle Island including, *The Malahat Review, Grain, CV2, TriQuarterly*,

The Fiddlehead, ARC Poetry Magazine, Best Canadian Poetry, Best New Poetry from the Midwest, and *Belt.* Along the way his work has garnered numerous Pushcart Prize nominations, National Magazine Award nominations, and Best of the Net nominations. He is pùkuwànkoamim̈ens of the Moravian of the Thames First Nation. Lockhart currently resides at Waawiiyaatanong and Pelee Island where he is the publisher at Urban Farmhouse Press.

Conal Smiley was born in London, Ontario. His childhood was spent combing the aisles of bookstores, video stores and record shops, which is where his passion for the arts began. He is mostly self-taught, and after some creative writing classes at U of T, he decided to pursue poetry. He currently lives in Toronto and works in bookstores. He has two chapbooks coming out late 2024/early 2025, on above/ground press and espresso.

Nina Jane Drystek is a poet, writer and performer based in Ottawa, unceded Algonquin Anishinaabe territory. she is author of *a:of:in* (Gap Riot Press, 2021) and *knewro suite* (Simulacrum Press, 2019), and her poems have appeared in online and print publications, as well as in self-published chapbooks and broadsides. her original sound poem scores can be heard on bandcamp. she is one of the co-founders of Riverbed Reading Series, was shortlisted for the 2020 Bronwen Wallace Award for Poetry, writes collaborative poetry with VII—authors of *holy disorder of being* (Gap Riot, 2022) and *Towers* (Collusion Books, 2021)—and performs sound poetry with the rotating group of collaborators. if you have ever lived in the same city as her you have likely seen her riding a red or blue bicycle. you can find her @textcurious or contact her via electronic mail.

Kathryn Mockler is the author of *Anecdotes* (Book*hug Press 2023), which won the 2024 Victoria Butler Book Prize and was a finalist for the 2024 Trillium Book Award, 2023 Danuta Gleed Literary Award, 2024 Fred Kerner Award, and 2024 VMI Besty Warland Between Genres Award. She co-edited the print anthology, *Watch Your Head: Writers and Artists Respond to the Climate Crisis* (Coach House Books, 2020) and runs the literary newsletter, *Send My Love to Anyone.*

Karen Houle is a Canadian poet and academic. She is most noted for her 2019 poetry collection, *The Grand River Watershed: A Folk Ecology*, which was a shortlisted finalist for the Governor General's Award for English-language poetry in 2019. A retired philosophy professor at the University of Guelph, she previously published the poetry collections *Ballast* (2000) and *During* (2005).

Fiona Tinwei Lam has authored three poetry collections and a children's book. She edited *The Bright Well: Contemporary Canadian Poems about Facing Cancer,* and co-edited two nonfiction anthologies. Shortlisted for the City of Vancouver Book Prize and other awards, her work appears in over 48 anthologies, including *Best Canadian Poetry* and *Best Canadian Essays.* She has collaborated on award-winning poetry videos that have screened at festivals internationally. She was Vancouver's poet laureate from 2022 to 2024.

Dominik Parisien is a disabled, queer FrenchCanadian writer and award-winning editor. He is the author of the poetry collection *Side Effects May Include Strangers* (McGill-Queen's University Press 2020) and a forthcoming memoir from Penguin Canada. He lives in Ottawa, ON.

Brandon Wint is an Ontario-born poet and multi-disciplinary storyteller based in Vancouver. For more than a decade, Brandon has been a sought-after performance poet, having shared his work all over Canada, and internationally at festivals and showcases in the United States, Australia, Jamaica, Latvia and Lithuania. Brandon Wint's poems and essays have been published in *The Ex-Puritan, Event Magazine, Arc Poetry Magazine,* and *Black Writers Matter,* among other places. *Divine Animal* (Write Bloody North 2020) was his debut collection of poetry.

Grace is a Hong Kong-born settler living on the traditional and Treaty territory of the Anishinabek people, now known as the Chippewa Tri-Council comprised of the Beausoleil, Rama, and Georgina Island First Nations. Her debut poetry collection, *The Language We Were Never Taught to Speak* (Guernica Editions 2021), is a Lambda Literary Award finalist.

Rasiqra Revulva is a queer femme writer, multimedia artist, editor, musician, performer and SciComm advocate. She is an editor of the climate crisis anthology *Watch Your Head: A Call to Action,* and one half of the experimental electronic duo The Databats (Slice Records, Melbourne; Toronto). She has published two chapbooks of glitch-illustrated poetry: *Cephalopography* (words(on)pages press 2016) and *If You Forget the Whipped Cream, You're No Good As A Woman* (Gap Riot Press 2018). *Cephalopography 2.0* was her debut collection. Learn more at @rasiqra_revulva, @thedatabats and www.rasiqrarevulva.com.

Hollay Ghadery is a multi-genre writer living in Ontario on Anishinaabe land. *Fuse,* her memoir of mixed-race identity and mental health, was released by Guernica Editions in 2021 and won the 2023 Canadian Bookclub Award for Nonfiction/Memoir. Her collection of poetry, *Rebellion Box* was released by Radiant Press in 2023, and her collection of short fiction, *Widow Fantasies,* was released with Gordon Hill Press in fall 2024. Hollay is the Poet Laureate of Scugog Township. Learn more about Hollay at www.hollayghadery.com.